They Call Her Lavender

Victoria Anne D'Anna

BookLeaf Publishing

India | USA | UK

Presentation by *BookLeaf Publishing*

www.bookleafpub.com

info@bookleafpub.com

ISBN: 978-93-5744-902-1

First edition 2021

To the boy who said I couldn't,

I can and I did.

Acknowledgements

Thank you for reading these words and giving them meaning. Without you, they mean nothing.

Mom, who has always been my biggest fan. I'm yours too. I love you and I'm forever grateful.

John, who taught me what having a great Dad is. I love you.

Gma, who has the kindest heart and the most resilient mind. You promised me 130 la ma.

Gpa, who was a man of few words, but taught me many. I think about you all the time.

Jake, who listens to every idea and helps make them better. I love you.

Hayley, who helped design a lovely cover for this book and is an even lovelier friend.

The rest of my family, who always encourage me to keep pursuing my art and supporting me along the way.

My friends (old and new), who always share my excitement and bring the best energy.

there is enough room for everyone and since
we are all here
move over and slide in another chair

- *make room*

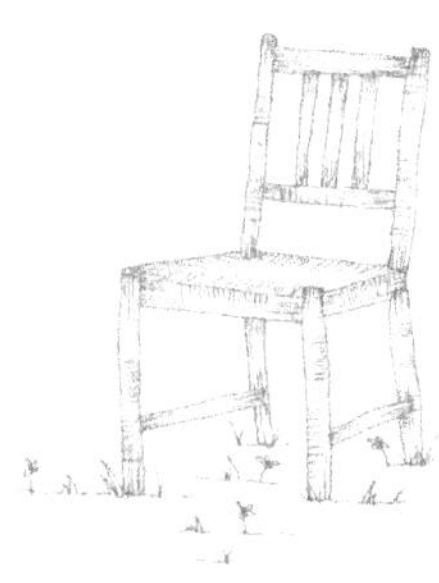

have we settled for poetry because we won't
make time for novels

- rush hour

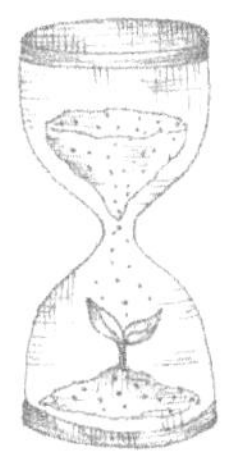

do not apologize for outgrowing other
people
you are a flower while they are a weed
their invasiveness rooted so deep
plant yourself where there is more room to
grow

- *growing apart*

trust your gut they said
he is such a nice guy they said
he loves you they said
he is just being protective they said
I should have listened to the first thing they
said

- stomach pains

instead of building me up you orchestrated
the demolition
every brick and stone of my body collapsed
into the earth
a cloud of dust burning your lungs and
making your eyes water
I will not rebuild a house
I will rebuild a palace
with a new lock on the door

- under construction

I made my body a life vest to keep you from
sinking
while I was busy saving you
you were making me drown

- save yourself first

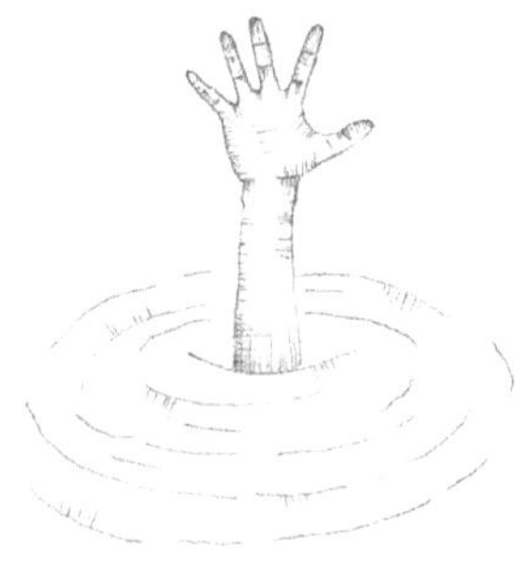

it is difficult to know a honey bee from a
wasp
one so sweet the earth cannot live without
the other greets with a bitter sting
instead of learning their differences
we have learned to treat them as the same

- *save the bees*

I want to be your sky
but I'm just a cloud in it
I catch your attention for a moment
I look like a fish, or maybe a rabbit
you think my presence brings rain
but I am only protecting you from the sun
I catch your attention for a moment
I look like a sailboat, or maybe a dragon
and just as fast I dissipate
it's clear skies again

- pareidolia

you stroked my spine with your finger
but didn't bother to read what was inside
you tore out my pages like my words were
irrelevant
I didn't need you to read me like a book
when I am a library

- illiterate

you would think butterflies and moths would
be treated as equals
but butterflies are met with beauty
and moths are deemed the culprit for the
hole in your favourite sweater

- *unbalanced*

crystals in my pocket
candles lit
white sage in abalone shells
lavender sprigs
you tried to burn me at the stake
but you choked on my smoke
a good witch a bad bitch

- *new magic*

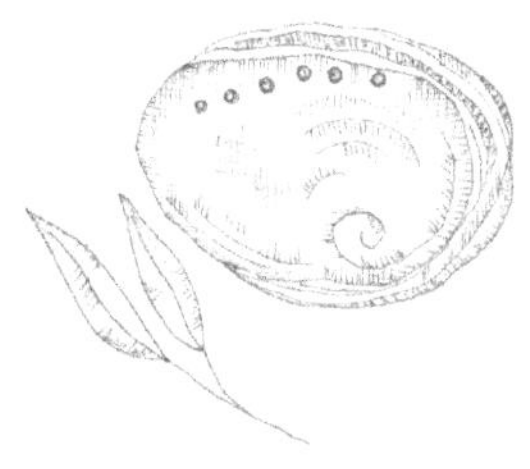

missing you is okay
going back to you is not

- moving forward

everyone wants to be touched by magic
but when it sprinkles down on us like
stardust
we are too stubborn to believe it's real

- a fairy died

it is a constant battle of feeling like a paper
just a hair too large for its envelope
you debate trimming the edge or folding it
with a harsh crease
compromising the paper's integrity to make
it fit just right
you force the paper into the envelope and
seal it shut

- *outgrown*

she met a boy who denied her sunlight and
wilted her leaves
she met a boy who watered her like rain
she quenched her thirst and bound herself to
the earth
an unstoppable force

- product of your environment

it's enchanting the way the earth breaks
through cracks in the pavement
little bits of green making their presence
known
tiny feats telling the world
"I'm not going anywhere"

- thriving

if you got through high school
you can get through anything

- *fact*

her two lips spoke the language of flowers
a soft whisper travelling in the rustle of
silvery-green foliage
her words resilient to winter's frost
she danced like an amethyst glinting in the
light
her body moving intuitively with the wind
she smelled of opulence and devotion
they bottled her up
and used a crown as the stopper

- they call her lavender

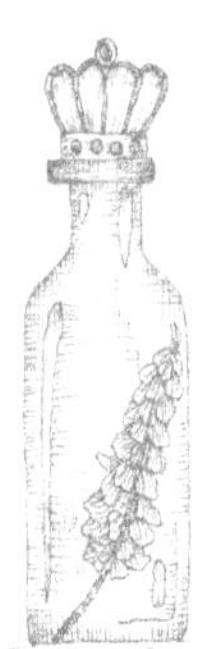

you're so beautiful when you've washed
away the stress of yesterday
a towel wrapped around your waist
your face warm and pink from the hot steam
water droplets collected in the crevice of
your collarbone
I wish our mornings didn't turn into
afternoons

- *sundays*

we construct wings out of paper and write
words to make them fly
we send off these little butterflies with
scribbles on their wings
in hopes their words find love
but sometimes during flight words lose their
meaning
and instead of finding us love
it makes us forget love ever existed at all

- paper wings

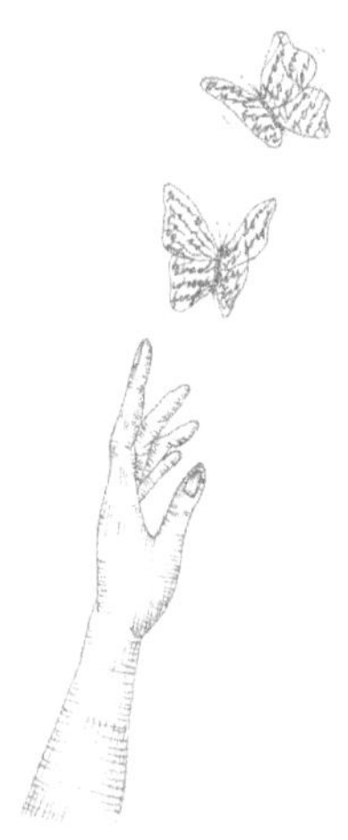

you smelled of espresso and cheap cigarettes
you didn't talk much then and you don't talk
much now
somehow, I always knew what you wanted
to say
you spoke of the silver house
with shingles made of garnets and sapphires
hidden away waiting patiently for me to find
it
I hope to find you instead

- when he visited